Guide in a tour to the watering places, and their environs, on the south-east coast of Devon.

William. Hyett

PRINT EDITIONS

Guide in a tour to the watering places, and their environs, on the south-east coast of Devon.
Hyett, William.
ESTCID: T193301
Reproduction from British Library
Anonymous. By William Hyett. With an additional undated titlepage which attributes the work to Hyett: 'A description of the watering places on the south-east coast of Devon, from the River Exe to the Dart inclusive, .. By W. Hyett. With a sketch of their
Exeter : printed by Trewman and Son, [1800?]
[2],105,[1]p.,plates ; 12°

Eighteenth Century
Collections Online
Print Editions

Gale ECCO Print Editions

Relive history with *Eighteenth Century Collections Online*, now available in print for the independent historian and collector. This series includes the most significant English-language and foreign-language works printed in Great Britain during the eighteenth century, and is organized in seven different subject areas including literature and language; medicine, science, and technology; and religion and philosophy. The collection also includes thousands of important works from the Americas.

The eighteenth century has been called "The Age of Enlightenment." It was a period of rapid advance in print culture and publishing, in world exploration, and in the rapid growth of science and technology – all of which had a profound impact on the political and cultural landscape. At the end of the century the American Revolution, French Revolution and Industrial Revolution, perhaps three of the most significant events in modern history, set in motion developments that eventually dominated world political, economic, and social life.

In a groundbreaking effort, Gale initiated a revolution of its own: digitization of epic proportions to preserve these invaluable works in the largest online archive of its kind. Contributions from major world libraries constitute over 175,000 original printed works. Scanned images of the actual pages, rather than transcriptions, recreate the works *as they first appeared.*

Now for the first time, these high-quality digital scans of original works are available via print-on-demand, making them readily accessible to libraries, students, independent scholars, and readers of all ages.

For our initial release we have created seven robust collections to form one the world's most comprehensive catalogs of 18th century works.

Initial Gale ECCO Print Editions collections include:

History and Geography
Rich in titles on English life and social history, this collection spans the world as it was known to eighteenth-century historians and explorers. Titles include a wealth of travel accounts and diaries, histories of nations from throughout the world, and maps and charts of a world that was still being discovered. Students of the War of American Independence will find fascinating accounts from the British side of conflict.

Social Science

Delve into what it was like to live during the eighteenth century by reading the first-hand accounts of everyday people, including city dwellers and farmers, businessmen and bankers, artisans and merchants, artists and their patrons, politicians and their constituents. Original texts make the American, French, and Industrial revolutions vividly contemporary.

Medicine, Science and Technology

Medical theory and practice of the 1700s developed rapidly, as is evidenced by the extensive collection, which includes descriptions of diseases, their conditions, and treatments. Books on science and technology, agriculture, military technology, natural philosophy, even cookbooks, are all contained here.

Literature and Language

Western literary study flows out of eighteenth-century works by Alexander Pope, Daniel Defoe, Henry Fielding, Frances Burney, Denis Diderot, Johann Gottfried Herder, Johann Wolfgang von Goethe, and others. Experience the birth of the modern novel, or compare the development of language using dictionaries and grammar discourses.

Religion and Philosophy

The Age of Enlightenment profoundly enriched religious and philosophical understanding and continues to influence present-day thinking. Works collected here include masterpieces by David Hume, Immanuel Kant, and Jean-Jacques Rousseau, as well as religious sermons and moral debates on the issues of the day, such as the slave trade. The Age of Reason saw conflict between Protestantism and Catholicism transformed into one between faith and logic -- a debate that continues in the twenty-first century.

Law and Reference

This collection reveals the history of English common law and Empire law in a vastly changing world of British expansion. Dominating the legal field is the *Commentaries of the Law of England* by Sir William Blackstone, which first appeared in 1765. Reference works such as almanacs and catalogues continue to educate us by revealing the day-to-day workings of society.

Fine Arts

The eighteenth-century fascination with Greek and Roman antiquity followed the systematic excavation of the ruins at Pompeii and Herculaneum in southern Italy; and after 1750 a neoclassical style dominated all artistic fields. The titles here trace developments in mostly English-language works on painting, sculpture, architecture, music, theater, and other disciplines. Instructional works on musical instruments, catalogs of art objects, comic operas, and more are also included.

The BiblioLife Network

This project was made possible in part by the BiblioLife Network (BLN), a project aimed at addressing some of the huge challenges facing book preservationists around the world. The BLN includes libraries, library networks, archives, subject matter experts, online communities and library service providers. We believe every book ever published should be available as a high-quality print reproduction; printed on-demand anywhere in the world. This insures the ongoing accessibility of the content and helps generate sustainable revenue for the libraries and organizations that work to preserve these important materials.

The following book is in the "public domain" and represents an authentic reproduction of the text as printed by the original publisher. While we have attempted to accurately maintain the integrity of the original work, there are sometimes problems with the original work or the micro-film from which the books were digitized. This can result in minor errors in reproduction. Possible imperfections include missing and blurred pages, poor pictures, markings and other reproduction issues beyond our control. Because this work is culturally important, we have made it available as part of our commitment to protecting, preserving, and promoting the world's literature.

GUIDE TO FOLD-OUTS MAPS and OVERSIZED IMAGES

The book you are reading was digitized from microfilm captured over the past thirty to forty years. Years after the creation of the original microfilm, the book was converted to digital files and made available in an online database.

In an online database, page images do not need to conform to the size restrictions found in a printed book. When converting these images back into a printed bound book, the page sizes are standardized in ways that maintain the detail of the original. For large images, such as fold-out maps, the original page image is split into two or more pages

Guidelines used to determine how to split the page image follows:

• Some images are split vertically; large images require vertical and horizontal splits.
• For horizontal splits, the content is split left to right.
• For vertical splits, the content is split from top to bottom.
• For both vertical and horizontal splits, the image is processed from top left to bottom right.

GUIDE

TO THE

WATERING PLACES

On the COAST of DEVON.

Price 2s. 6d.

Guide

IN A TOUR

TO THE

WATERING PLACES,

And their ENVIRONS,

ON THE SOUTH-EAST COAST OF DEVON.

"O nature, how in every charm supreme!
Whose votaries feast on raptures ever new!
O! for the voice and fire of Seraphim
To sing thy glories with devotion due."

MINSTREL

EXETER

PRINTED BY TREWMAN AND SON, HIGH STREET.

103 58 644 12

A

DESCRIPTION

OF THE

WATERING PLACES

Of the SOUTH EAST COAST of DEVON,

From the River EXE to the DART inclusive,

COMPREHENDING

DAWLISH, TEIGNMOUTH, SHALDON, and TORQUAY.

By W HYETT

WITH A

SKETCH OF THEIR LOCAL HISTORY;

and a Four te and correct Account of NOBLEMEN'S and
GENTLEMEN'S SEATS, and Objects in the Vicinage of
each, worthy the Attention of the Antiquary, and
Admirer of Picturesque and Romantic Scenery

—>eeeee—

Embellished with FOUR ETCHINGS

EXETER

Printed and sold by TREWMAN and SON, Fore street
Sold also by CADELL and DAVIES, Strand, London, and all other
Booksellers

ADVERTISEMENT

———————

THE design of the following pages, is to lay before the stranger, in the first instance, the state of each of the watering places mentioned in the title, with a description of their environs, to enable him to determine WHICH shall be his place of SEJOUR, during the summer months, and in the next, when fixed in his choice, to point out, and assist him in exploring, the objects that are worthy his attention in the vicinity.

Where the design has been fulfilled, the Author feels it his duty to ascribe the merit to those Gentlemen who have favoured him with their remarks

and

and affiſtance; eſpecially to one,* to whom he is particularly grateful.

The ſcenery of DEVON, (particularly this part of the coaſt) altho' it has had the honor of a viſit from ſome eminent touriſts, has been too curſorily inſpected,—is far from being generally known,—and has even been deſcribed as wanting thoſe traits of pictureſque beauty, with which other diſtricts abound, from this imputation it is but juſtice to attempt to reſcue it.

Few counties can boaſt of having theſe qualities in a higher degree than Devonſhire, but (as elſewhere) they do not always occur in turnpike roads To diſcover the charms of NATURE, we muſt follow her ſteps thro' the wild glen, by the foaming river, and aſcend the ſteep hill, clad with luxuriant foliage, to where the ſcathed rock riſes from the romantic eminence in rugged majeſty, all the diverſities of which may be found even in the limited

* Rev Mr Swete, of Oxton-houſe

mited ride of one day, from the places before-mentioned, besides the rich and more cultivated scenery,
of the various seats and villas that decorate the
face of the country

The etchings that accompany the work, are merely
given as sketches, and may serve to convey a better
idea of the place described.

DAWLISH.

DAWLISH.

―――

" O Dawlish, though unclaffic be thy name,
By every mufe unfung, fhould from thy tide,
To keen poetic eyes alone reveal'd,
From the cerulean bofom of the deep
(As Aphrodite rofe of old) appear
Health's blooming goddefs, and benignant fmile
On her true votary, not Cythera s fame,
Not Eryx, nor the laurel boughs which waved
On Delos erft, Apollo's natal foil,
However warm, enthufiaftic youth
Dwelt on thofe feats enamour d, fhall to me
Be half fo dear   To thee will I confign
Often the timid virgin, to thy pure
Incircling waves, to thee will I confign
The feeble matron, or the child on whon
Thou may ft beftow a fecond happier birth,
From weaknefs into ftrength   And fhould I view
Unfetter d, with the found firm judging mind,
Imagination to return, array'd
In her once glowing veft, to thee my lyre
Shall oft be tun'd, and to thy Nereids green,
Long, long unnoticed in their haunts retired
Nor will I ceafe to prize thy lovely ftrand,
Thy towering clifls, nor the fmall babling brook,
Whofe fhallow current laves thy thiftled vale. '
                    Downman s Infancy.

A 1   DAWLISH,

DAWLISH, (anciently *Dawlish*) is said to derive its name from *Dol-es*, "a fruitful mead in a bottom," or, "on a river's side." It has, within a *few* years, grown from an inconsiderable fishing cove, to its present state of improvement and elegance. At first it was frequented by those for whom the gaieties of EXMOUTH and TEIGNMOUTH had no charms, and, by degrees, in consequence of the salubrity of its air, the convenience it affords for bathing, and its natural beauties, becoming better known, it has justly acquired much reputation

DAWLISH is charmingly situated in a valley, environed by high grounds on all sides but the east, where the ever-varying ocean spreads its cerulean expanse, fronting which, on the strand, are some good lodging-houses, connected with the cliff, higher, on the hill, are five or six other buildings, well calculated for the residence of genteel families, proudly overlooking

looking those below, yet conveniently retired, having a small shrubbery in front, judiciously contrived to screen the obtruding chimnies. The most conspicuous object from this part, however, is a structure erected by Sir *Henry Watson*, after the Gothic style of architecture, exhibiting, in front, a kind of arcade, with columns and pointed arches, decorated with escutcheons and fret-work pinnacles, forming one of the most pleasing specimens of the Gothic manner; it stands, surrounded by a garden, stored with a variety of exotic plants, on one of the cliffs, overlooking the shore for a considerable way, with its huge craggy, and separated rocks, commanding the view of Teignmouth, and looking into the opening of Torbay. Nearer the sea, a whimsical mount, in imitation of the natural rock, has been raised, formed into a cell on the inside. Farther up the vale, a row of neat dwellings present themselves, among which are to be distinguished the two inns, each professing to-

rable accommodations. The grift-mill oppofite, fo fingularly fituate, and picturefque,
feldom fails of attracting the ftranger of more
than common obfervation· it is an overfhot-
mill, and the ftream falling over a ledge of
gravel, ere it comes to the wheel, gives a romantic air to the fcene, above this, where the
valley becomes contracted, fix or eight genteel
lodging-houfes are fituate, fronting the fea,
having each a fmall plot before them, inclofed
with neat railing   From hence to the church,
the diftance is half a mile, on either fide the
road, there are ftraggling cottages, that form a
fort of connexion between the places, contiguous to the bridge are two good and pleafant
houfes, near which appears another mill, where
the fcenery is alfo very pleafing, the building
itfelf is fimple and well difpofed, the winding
road, and the trees intermingling themfelves,
have a good effect, while the light poplars beyond, and the bell cupola of the manor-houfe,*

give

* Rented by Captain Schanks, but the property of J.
Inglett Fortefcue, Efq.

give a grace of elegance   Oppofite the laft-mentioned houfe, ftands that of Mr. *Churchill*, a very neat building, neai which is fituate the chuich, a handfome Gothic ftructure, fui-rounded by elm rows of confideiable fize, the fouth front is very fine,——between each of the ramified windows there is a nich, in fome of which are the remains of mutilated ftatues, and in a nich at the eaft end, is one that has received no injury fiom the fanatics, who probably, in the civil wars of King Chailes the Firft, deftroyed the ieft. The walls aie crefted with battlements, and ornamented with pinnacles   Neaily at the eaft end iifes a pio-jecting turret, (which feives as a ftaircafe to the ioof) pinnacled alfo, and of elegant archi-tecture

The vicaiage-houfe ftands enclofed by its gaidens, which boift a natuialization, as it were of exotics, that elfewheie require the

foftering

foftering hand of art It is fheltered from the
north by a high hill, and a fcreen of elms de-
fends it from the weftern blafts

DAWLISH has no regular market, tho' it is
tolerably well fupplied with animal food, vegetables, &c by the neighbourhood, and an
opportunity offers of fending by the *Teignmouth
coach*, that paffes through the village thrice times
a week to EXETER. The bathing machines are
numerous and well conducted, and the beach,
in front of the lodging-houfes defcends gently
into the fea, which is generally clean, and free
from weeds

The *Public Walk* extends in a ftraight line
over the ftrand, oppofite the interminable ocean,
and is kept in excellent repair, affording a
moft agreeable *promenade*, which may be length-
ened by a ftroll under the cliffs, that are here
of tremendous height, bold and precipitous,
though not of a very denfe and compact ftratum,

tum, as is evident from the incroachments which the furge, and its faline fpray, have made on them, and the huge fragments that lie fcattered at their feet, from whence the mineralogift may, at times, collect fine fpecimens of iron-ore, in cluftered globules. Thro' a fiffure, not badly reprefenting a Gothic door, a paffage opens to a little beach below, of a fine and firm confiftence, where are fome grotefque maffes, which being of a more folid nature, have withftood the buffetings of the affailing element; while the intermediate body, of a loofer texture, has fuffered a decompofition, and been wafhed away.

RIDES.

A Tour to POWDERHAM, OXTON, MAMHEAD, *&c. Total diftance about* 14 *miles.*

As if unwilling to part with its vifitors, DAWLISH oppofes fatiguing hills for them to furmount,

mount, at either extremity Having gained
the fummit of that, leading to STARCROSS, we
have a view of the entrance to the EXE, the
cliffs near BUDLEIGH SALTERTON ;

"———— and the diftant coaft,
In mifts array'd, juft heaving into fight
Above the dim horizon, where the fail
Appears confpicuous in the lengthen'd gleam,"

and foon after, on the left, the fine eminence
of MANHEAD, with a fir plantation, beautifully hanging on the fide of a hill, from the
apex of which an obelifk fhoots up, and marks
the country.

Entering a fmall common, we leave the
STARCROSS road for that which branches to the
left, and which conducts us thro' a fhady lane
to the dilapidated chapel of COITON Thefe
ruins are feated above the road, and offer feveral good fcenes for the pencil, being richly
curtained with ivy, from the part that was
originally the chancel, (and even now contains
a monument) is a pretty vifta, thro' a Gothic
arch,

arch, and a breach in the end wall, of the diſtant country. The ſketch given fronts this chancel. Soon after leaving COFTON, we rejoin the *Starcroſs road*, at the ſod, ſouth-eaſt of which, ſeated on the beach beneath the high hills of *Cockwood*, is a pleaſant manſion, belonging to *Doctor Drury*, chief maſter of Harrow-ſchool, to whoſe taſte and agricultural enterprizes the country is indebted   On the left, are two of thoſe ornaments of DEVON which Mr. *Gilpin* well denominates " *lime-kiln caſtles;*" at the junction of theſe roads we catch a charming view of the noble river EXE, the town of EXMOUTH, with the handſome row of brick houſes on *Chapel-bill*; and *Marpool*, the ſeat of *W. Hull*, Eſq.—Starcroſs, which we now enter, is a charming village, ſituate on the bank of the river, which it overlooks, as well as the oppoſite ſhore. The inn we may rank among the moſt pleaſant of the houſes here, whoſe bow-window preſents a delightful proſpect of the ſwelling EXE, from the town of
TOPSHAM

TOPSHAM to its estuary. Pursuing our route on the banks, we are led to *Powderham-castle* the seat of *Lord Viscount Courtenay* This castle was probably first erected to repel and awe the invading Danes, who, before the conquest, made frequent incursions on this coast. It has, of course, undergone many alterations and improvements since that time, tho' it still appears to be an ancient structure. The hand of taste has swept away the wall that once inclosed a quadrangular court in front, with its heavy gate-way, and laid the house open to the park, which is well stocked with deer, and decorated with some beautiful clumps of oak, beech, chesnut, and walnut-trees Within its walls, the man of fashion will be amused by the elegant decorations, and the *amateurs* of pictures by works of the old masters, among which, the "tribute money of Rubens" is of superior excellence. The pleasure grounds are exceedingly fine and extensive, the shrubberies luxuriant, and the plantations flourishing. The

Belvidere,

Belvidere, erected by the late *Lord Courtenay*, is of a triangular form, with an hexagonal tower on each corner;—it commands a profpect of the lovely interchange of wooded heights and defcending vales, with the majeftic river Exe, rolling its congregated waters into the fwelling ocean, its variegated fhore from above Topsham to Exmouth, and the dark hills of Woodbury, with their fir-crowned fummits fkirting behind Croffing the canal by an elegant bridge, we quit *Powderham*, and pafs thro' the village, and near the handfome church of Kenton, about two miles from which is *Oxton-Houfe*, the feat of the *Rev. J. Swete*, the delightful and picturefque grounds of which abound with fcenery worthy the pencil of their proprietor, whofe claffic tafte has admirably difplayed itfelf, in the judicious ftyle the lucid ftream is taught to meander thro' the fertile vale, in the charming walks that permeate the noble woods; and in the various ornamental buildings that grace its romantic eminences

We

We enter this fairy scene by a venerable gateway, by which a cafcade foams violently over a huge mafs of ftones; oppofed to which is the clear expanfe of a tranquil lake, overfhadowed by fome luxuriant trees, thro' the floating foliage of which we behold the manfion-houfe, feated on a gently rifing lawn, this (as well as every part of the grounds) is indebted to the prefent poffeffor for the beauties and conveniencies it has to boaft. Tracing up the murmuring rivulet, beyond a ruftic bridge, we follow the windings of a path thro' the rich woods, and proceed on the heights to the *cottage*, a pleafuie-houfe, built in the Gothic ftyle, fecluded among fome fine oaks, round its walls the woodbine has hung its fragrant wreaths, which gives it an air of chafte fimplicity from its windows we are prefented with a charming tract of country,

> " Where palaces, and fanes, and villas rife,
> And gardens fmile around,"

with many a catch of the gleaming river, from

the

the walls of the city of EXETER to its union with
the ocean.* We now re-enter a wood, and
gain the gate that joins the public road, immediately oppofite which, another gate opens
into the extenfive lawns of *Mambead,* the
property of the *Earl of Lifburne,* which offer
to the eye a rich and uncloying banquet, its
pleafing undulations, and light verdure, relieved by rich maffes of fhadow, interpofed in
elegant variety. But the profpect this fpot commands is its chief boaft. *Powderham-caftle,*
with its various plantations, and the villages
that encircle it, are feen on this fide of the
river, which is alfo in full view, while the horizon difplays the hills of SOMERSET and DOR-
SETSHIRE, not far from the houfe, which is a
noble ftructure, and finely fituated, ftands the
picturefque church of *Mambead,* furrounded

by

---

* The feats of Bickham and Trehill have charms
enough to induce the traveller to continue his excurfion,
if agreeable. The grounds of each, befide their own
beauties, finely difplaying thofe of each other.

by fheltering trees, and is a charming ornament to the lawn. Above the houfe, on the
brow of HALDON, rifes a plantation of firs, many
of them of ftupendous fize, amid which towers
the ftately obelifk   As we advance

" ——————— Beneath the fhades
Of folemn oaks, that tuft the fwelling mounts,
Thrown graceful round by Nature's carelefs hand,"

we catch a glimpfe of *Mambead cottage*,
fweetly embofomed in rich foliage, and attended by thofe rural accompaniments which
fhould ever mark and characterife a cottage.
Having reached the extremity of thofe charming fcenes, where are to be remarked fome of
the fineft ilexes in the kingdom, we join a
road that leads before the parfonage-houfe of
Mambead, a modern building, feated high,
and poffeffing a moft extenfive view, yet defended from the rude blafts by rifing hills and
plantations, behind which we again view the
obelifk. The Ridge-way, on which we now

travel,

travel, is one of the moſt pleaſant roads in the weſt of ENGLAND, from its height.

> " The burſting proſpect ſpreads immenſe around,
> And ſnatched o'er hill and dale, and wood and lawn,
> And verdant fields, and darkening heaths between,
> And villages emboſom'd ſoft in trees,
> And ſpiry towns, by ſurging columns mark'd
> Of houſehold ſmoke, your eye excurſive roams "

Among the parts diſcriminated, are the neg-lected grounds of *New-houſe,* * well worth, however, the attention of thoſe who are ad-mirers of fine trees; for here will be found Spaniſh cheſnuts, oaks, and beech, eſpecially two of the latter, contiguous, not to be rivalled in the county   Having paſſed a direction poſt, we take the firſt lane to the right, and dip into a glen, following the courſe of a ri-vulet towards DAWLISH, the tower of which is ſeen gleaming thro' the hedge-row elms, and gaining another road, a gate to the right permits us a view of *Luſcombe*, a ſeat belong-

ing

---

* The property of Mr Oxenham, who has unfortu-nately laboured under mental derangement, for many years.

ing to Mr. *Hoare.* This is a handfome gothic edifice, decorated with battlements,* fituated in a verdant tho' narrow dale, furrounded by hills, which fo completely fhelter it from the bleak winds, that the climate muft be as foft and ferene as that of Cythera. Altho' the grounds are yet in an infant ftate, we cannot fail of noticing the beauty of a ruftic fhed, fronting a coppice that clothes the hill to the right as we enter. We proceed from hence, thro' the higher part of the village, to *Dawlifb Strand.*

Ride thro' ASHTON, &c. *to* FULFORD-HOUSE.
Total 22 *miles.*

We now trace up the fame vale, thro' which our laft route paffed, the road being conducted nearly on a level, for two or three miles, about

a

---

* The white bricks of which the battlements and chimnies are compofed, were invented and brought to perfection by James Templer, Efq

a gun-fhot above the plane of the valley, on the
declining fide of a hill. Nearly on the firft
entrance to *Afhcombe* parifh, in a fmall hamlet, is one of thofe picturefque mills found in
almoft every dell of this county. From this we
wind with the vale, whofe breadth fcarcely
extends to a furlong, and frequently fuffering
by the ravages of the ftream, to a bridge, which
is thrown acrofs it, and climb a fteep afcent,
by the church, to the heathy brow of HALDON,
croffing the barren heights of which, to the
weft, we foon view that magnificent edifice,
Haldon-Houfe, the refidence of Sir *Lawrence
Palk*, Bart. M. P. for the county of DEVON,
ftanding in an extenfive lawn, which is decorated with fome ftately clumps of trees, and
fheltered behind by fome flourifhing and wide
extending plantations, over which (on *Penhill*)
rifes *Lawrence Tower*, a confpicuous object
from all the country to a vaft diftance, the elegant room of which prefents views as fine and
grand as extenfive. From HALDON we dip
into

into the dell and village of ASHTON, paffing near a dilapidated manfion of the ancient family of the *Chudleighs* We are now in a country where every new afpect offers a fcene adapted for the pencil, the luxuriant growth of the mofs-clad trees, that hang on the hills; the rocky maffes, add to the charms of the flowing TEIGN, now before us, on the banks of which we journey, for two miles, to DUNSFORD, where the fame picturefque fcenery abounds,

" 'The dripping rock and mountain's mifty top
Swell on the fight,"

while the fine foliage of the oak overhangs the foaming river. Above this we find *Clifford-bridge*, which is alfo rich in woods, the hamlet beyond, and the hills, rifing in charming fucceffion, exhibit a moft attracting affemblage Before we reach the bridge, we diverge to the right, and afcending thro' a ftoney lane, are brought to *Great Fulford-Houfe*. The houfe confifts of a quadrangle, having a huge gateway, whereon is an efcutcheon, bearing the

arms

arms of the family of the *Fulfords*. We are informed that it suffered much during the great rebellion, when it was garrisoned on behalf of Charles the first. It has some excellent apartments, in which are some good paintings, particularly a portrait of king Charles, by Vandyke, said to have been taken after his Majesty's condemnation, and given to *Sir Francis Fulford*, as a testimony of royal approbation This mansion stands pleasantly on a gently rising ground, having some good avenues of beech round it, and a fine piece of water.

The romantic country thro' which we have already passed will not suffer by a retrospection, the picturesque beauties being not at all inferior, when taken in this point of view, to that already seen. Having gained the ascent of HALDON, (from whence there are some extensive views) we travel a few miles on the *Teignmouth-road,* and ere we reach the south-

B

eɩn extremity,* turning to the left, descend
to DAWLISH.

———

Ride from DAWLISH *to* TEIGNMOUTH,—3 *miles.*

Passing before the house of Mr *Churchill,* we
climb a steep hill, and having crossed a small
common, proceed thro' the little village of
HOLCOMBE, at the next dell beyond which we
enter a narrow lane to the left, and follow the
course of a small stream, (that falls into the
sea) which presents us with a very picturesque
waterfall, to the beauty of which the glen,
between the terminating cliffs, the disparted
fragments of the rock, and the ocean skirting
behind, greatly contributes. At a small distance to the east of the above, the sea has, by
beating hard against the promontory, worn the
cliffs

———

* Not far from this is a gate, opening into a narrow
lane leading to Ludwel Chapel, the ruins of which stand
in the lower angle of a field called Chapel Park, shrouded
with alders.

cliffs into caverns, and feparated the loofer parts from the more folid rock This is a diftinguifhing point, from the fingularity of a wide opening, like the arch of a ruftic bridge, and of a huge mafs of rock* that ftands detached as a pillar, amid the waves, from thence, if the tide permits, we fhall find a pleafant ride on the fands, which are of firm confiftence, or, returning to the public road, afcend the hill, from the apex of which we have a charming profpect of the rivers Exe and Teign, with a long ftretching coaft, loft at length in the blue horizon, and having paffed two or three genteel houfes, feated on the fide of a hill, and overlooking the town, defcend to Teignmouth

---

* Known by the name of the Parfon and Clerk.

TEIGNMOUTH

TEIGNMOUTH

DERIVES its name from its situation at the *embouchure* of the river TEIGN, to the source of which I beg leave to conduct the reader The TEIGN has its rise on the forest of DARTMOOR, near GIDLEIGH,—it was so called by the Britons, according to the best etymologists, " in that its stream was pent up between impassable barriers." The country thro' which it runs is uncommonly wild and romantic, especially in its infant state, when it enters *Gidleigh Park,* which it divides in two parts. The right bank (tracing it towards the sea) is covered by a venerable wood, interspersed with huge rocky fragments, and the bold hill that rises on the left, (in the possession of a colony of rabbits,) frequently presents hoary masses of granite,

protruding

protruding thro' the excavated furface This
fcenery continues, with little variation, to
CHAGFORD, near which is a bridge of three
arches over the ftream, finely vefted with ivy,
and accompanied by a moft picturefque view
of the well-foliaged heights and winding vale
Not far from CHAGFORD lies *Whiddon park*, a
defolate manfion, of little confequence, but
fituated on a fpot that boafts fome of the moft
enchanting rude pictures the hand of nature
ever finifhed. The rich encruftations of the
rocks,—the variegated tint of the moffes that
beautify the venerable trees, and render them
fo valuable to the painter, luxuriantly abound
in this neighbourhood. Nor fhould we omit
the fine fcenery of RUSHFORD,

" Where o'er the *rocks* the fcarcely waving *oak*
Fills the brown fhade with a religious awe "

at the foot of which the TEIGN foams with
great violence, its channel often interrupted
by large loofe ftones In the parifh of DREWS-
TEIGNTON, (fo named, it is conjectured, from

B 3   " being

" being the town of the *Druids* on the *Teign*."
And truly, the wild, retired, and awfully impreſ-
five ſcenes here found, ſuch as theſe formidable
prieſts always choſe for their ſuperſtitious rites,
independant of the many *druidical remains* ſtill
extant, favour the etymology,) oppoſite *Whiddon park*, is to be ſeen the *Logan-ſtone* It lies
in the ſubject of our preſent diſquiſition and
had, as appears by the teſtimony of the neighbourhood, an oſcillatory motion, ſome years
ſince, but it is now immoveable * Below this
is *Fingal bridge*, the ſcenery round which is de-
licious, vaſt rocks of granite, adorned with
the fine foliage of the oak, of the moſt fan-
taſtic forms, here and there overhung with ivy
and mountain ſhrubs, with the rapid ſtream,
conſpire to form a ſeries of ſtudies, worthy a
painter at the head of his profeſſion Not far
from *Fingal bridge*, (on *Preſton farm*,) are the

remains

* At no great diſtance from hence, on the left bank
of the Teign, ſtands one of thoſe Britiſh monuments,
the Cromlech.

remains of a camp, commonly attributed to the Danes From thence the river divides the parishes of DUNSFORD and BRIDFORD, whose bold hills still retain the same clothing On the right bank, in the parish of CHRISTOW, is situate an old pile of building, now going to decay, belonging to *William Helyar*, Esq —*Canonteign*, so called from its having been attached to the priory of Black Canons, of *Merton, Surry*, some of the rooms still retain their original form and dimensions. It is, at this time, inhabited by a farmer, below it, is a huge mass of moorstone, named, from its contiguity, *Canonteign rock*, by which a waterfall dashes furiously

———— " Beneath the precipice,
Amidst encircling groves, from cliff to cliff"

and rushing down the dell, soon joins the TEIGN, the banks are now more cultivated tho' many a brown coppice still crowns the neighbouring eminences, untill the stream is crossed by *Chudleigh bridge*, above which stands *Stole-*

lake,

lake, a houfe re-building on the fcite of the old one. The landfcape from hence is moft delightful, having *Chudleigh rock* full in view, and the charming meanders of the river, which, below *New-bridge,* is united with the waters of the *Weft Teign,* or *Bovey river,* and thro' fertile meadows proceeds to TEIGNBRIDGE, over which the turnpike road from EXETER to NEWTON BUSHEL paffes, and gradually widening its congregated ftreams, receives the canal (a work of great utility to the neighbourhood) at " *the marfh,*" fomewhat more than half a mile diftant from NEWTON BUSHEL, and is navigable for barges, and other fmall craft, from thence to TEIGNMOUTH, and thro' a narrow gut, under the *Ne/s,* difcharges itfelf into the fea At its mouth it has difgorged fuch an immenfe body of fand, (accumulating thro' a fucceffion of years) as to render it impaffable, for veffels of any defcription, at low water.

TEIGNMOUTH,

TEIGNMOUTH, unlike many modern water-ing places, (the fortuitous growth of a few years,) may, from a variety of circumstances, contend for the palm, with the most distin-guished of them, and has to boast not only ancient, but *eventful* history, in the chronicles of *other times* It is divided into two parishes, EAST-TEIGNMOUTH and WEST-TEIGNMOUTH, separated from each other by a small brook called the *Tame* Cambden dates the arrival of the Danes (who were sent to discover the situ-ation of BRITAIN) in the year 800, but *Risdon* protracts it for nearly two centuries. On their landing here they defeated the natives, and killed the kings lieutenant, which these ban-ditti considered as a most favourable presage of future victory, and penetrating farther into the country, ravaged it to a considerable ex-tent. Nor have the Danes been the only foes to TEIGNMOUTH,—it was plundered, and partly burnt, by the French, in later times;—it was then, however, a very poor place, compared

B 5

with

with its appearance at the prefent day ,—but, like the *Phœnix*, it arofe with fuperior beauty from its afhes The brief that was originally made and collected for the relief of the dif- treffed people and for re-building the part deftroyed, is ftill in being One of the new- erected ftreets was named *French-ftreet*, as a memorial of the unfortunate circumftance.

TEIGNMOUTH is diftant about fourteen miles from EXETER , and is well fheltered from the north and north-eaft winds by rifing hills, *at,* or rather *near* the foot of which, being partly on a gentle declivity, it ftands, having the pleafant village of SHALDON in front, the be- fore-mentioned river on the weft, and the wide expanfe of ocean on the eaft The com- merce of TEIGNMOUTH confifts chiefly of the ex- portation of *pipe,* or more properly *potter's* clay, to STAFFORDSHIRF, LIVERPOOL, &c (which clay is brought moftly from the vicinage of TEIGN- BRIDGE, and from the lands of *James Templer,* Efq.

Efq of *Stover Lodge*, at whofe fole expence the before-noticed canal was cut, and to whofe patriotic exertions the country and trade are particularly indebted,) the importation of coals, and the *Newfoundland trade*,—in which latter SHALDON alfo participates The veffels employed in taking the commodities to their refpective markets, are built here. TEIGN-MOUTH has two inns,—the *Globe*, from whence a coach fets off thrice times a week, paffing thro' DAWLISH and STARCROSS to EXETER, and returns the fame evening and *Hubbard's Hotel*, both poffeffing good accommodations From *Hubbard's billiard room* you have a delight-ful and extenfive view up the river, which, under a calm fky, when the tide is in, appears like a magnificent lake, while the clay barges, whofe forms are truly picturefque, and many a light fkiff cruifing to and fro, animate the water, and mark its receffion The country on each fide of the river is well adapted to the fcene, and at the back, *Ingfdon*, the beautiful

B 6

feat

feat of Mrs *Hale*, and *Highweek church*, gleam thro' the circumjacent trees, while the hill that terminates the profpect is crowned by a romantic rock.

WEST-TEIGNMOUTH had formerly a charter for a market, held on a Sunday, which continued to the time of Henry the Third, when the Sheriff's poffe forced them to difcontinue the irreligious practice altogether There is, however, a market for poultry, butcher's meat, butter, &c. every Saturday, with which it is tolerably well fupplied, vegetables and fruit alfo, when in feafon, may be procured in abundance Salmon, falmon-peal, fea-trout, whiting, mackerel, and feveral other fpecies of fifh are taken here, and, by an excellent local regulation, the inhabitants are allowed to fupply themfelves before any is fold to the dealers There are feveral good houfes here,— *Teignmouth-houfe*, the refidence of *J Baring*, Efq late Member of Parliament for EXETER,

claims

claims our first attention;—it commands fine
and extensive prospects from its bow windows :
and *Bitton,* the seat of *Mackworth Praed,* Esq.
enjoys nearly similar views   Above the church
stands Mrs. *Boscawen's cottage,* which, from the
singularity of its various decorations, has at-
tracted general notice   *West-Teignmouth church*
is a cruciform building, near the centre of the
town,—seen from the opposite side of the
river, the tower, which is destitute of battlements, appears to be much higher than it **really**
is   The roof of this church is supported in a
peculiar manner by the ramifications **of a**
wooden pillar that runs up in the middle —
The interior contains two good galleries, and
several neat monuments,—altho' these tablets
are in general made up either of pompous
enumerations of the virtues of the deceased,
or are expressed in such language as moves
risibility rather than excites serious reflec-
tion, yet I must beg leave to introduce one,
free from fulsome eulogy, and breathing an affectionate

fectionate regret for a deceased child   It is
erected to the memory of *Mary Foote*, daughter
of the *Rev. H Foote*, of *Charlton-place, Kent* ———

"Endowed by Providence with an excellent understanding and affectionate heart, which were
cherished and improved by diligent cultivation.
She had always given a most promising earnest
of mature virtues, when it pleased the Almighty,
at an early period, to terminate her severe pro-
bation   Her patience and humble resignation
to the divine will, thro' a long and painful ill-
nefs, endeared her to her afflicted friends, her
fervent, yet rational piety, has left them nothing to lament but their own lofs"

Enclofed in frames, are extracts from the wills
of Sir *J Elwill* and Sir *I. Elwill*, his fon, containing an account of their donations, to be
applied to the laudable purpofe of educating
poor children of both parifhes   This church is an
appendage to the living of BISHOPSTEIGNTON.

EAST-TEIGNMOUTH is the grand refort of
gaiety and fafhion, and, as it is faid, was a
borough that vied with EXETER for antiquity.

Here

Here you taste the pure air, and enjoy an uninterrupted view of the ocean, and " its changeful scenery ever new." Here the best lodging-houses are situate, and may be hired, furnished or unfurnished, at the option of the tenant, and here stand the *Public Rooms*, a neat brick building, affording an agreeable lounge, it contains tea, coffee, assembly and billiard rooms, and a ball is held here once every fortnight or three weeks, in the beginning of the season, and more frequent as it advances

A *theatre* has been lately erected on a spot of ground given for the purpose by *Lord Viscount Courtenay*, and has been opened for the reception of the audience this summer — The *bathing machines* are well contrived and attended, and the beach composed of a soft carpet of sand, with here and there a layer of small pebbles, slopes gradually into the sea, which is generally very clear, free from weeds, and sheltered from all but the east wind. Near the

beach

beach is *East-Teignmouth church*,—this venerable pile will, of courfe, attract the ftrangers notice, the ftyle of its architecture carries its foundation back to the earlieft periods of chriftianity, and, with probability, it may be referred to the Saxons. The round tower, connected with the fquare one,—the windows narrow, with femicircular arches,—and the corbels, (heads of men or animals, placed as ornamental fupports to the parapet) are marks of a Saxon, or, at the loweft, of a Norman origin There is a ftriking fimilarity in the architecture of this church and that of *Bifhopfteignton*,—the towers are nearly alike, and many circumftances confpire to prove the period of the foundation of that fine old ftructure to be nearly coeval with it The infide of the building however is dark and inconvenient It appertains to *Dawlifh church* in like manner as *Weft-Teignmouth* does to *Bifhopfteignton* The minifter is nominated by the joint concurrence of the two paftors, and ferves the parifhes alternately

WALKS

WALKS

" *The Walk*," as it is ftyled, leads from the *public rooms* towards the fouth, over an extenfive flat called the *Den*, *(Dena terræ*, a low flat between hills) on which ftands the fort, whofe cannon, of whatever fervice they may prove in defending the town, may, on gala days, join their roar with the general explofions of tumultuous applaufe. The *Den* is compofed of fine fand, interfperfed with large patches of a fort of grafs that affumes a fimilar hue, and harmonizes finely with its brown particles Here the inhabitants ufually *promenade*, and breathe the unadulterated air, for whofe accommodation there are feats placed in agreeable fituations, from hence you may enjoy a view of the fea, with the tall cliffs and undulating curve of *Babicombe Bay*, ending in a point called *Hope's Nofe*, the coaft to the north-eaft, comprehending Exmouth and Sidmouth, to Lyme; the fine profpeÉt up the river, whofe fweeping lines

are

are fkirted by many little hamlets, and the fhipping in the eftuary, to which we may add, the affemblage of beauty and elegance a fummer's evening generally draws to the fpot — Among the fcenes worthy the attention of a minute obferver, that of *fean drawing* is not the leaft amufing,—it is performed by women, habited for the purpofe, on whofe countenances, as the centre of the net approaches the fhore, expectation fits triumphant, fhould the draught prove fuccefsful, the clamour is univerfal; but if, alas! they get " an empty haul," they drop the net, and the whole group filently fteal off to their refpective boats   Nor fhould we pafs over the fmall fleets of fifhing barks that arrive here every morning,—the anxious crowd of buyers that wait their return,—nor the paffage boats, with their freights, that continually ply to and fro, and agreeably diverfify the fcene

A very pleafing walk leads to the weftward of the town, by the fine grove near *Bitton*, on

the

the turnpike road, and banks of the river, which may be varied by a return beneath the road, on the fands, at the receffion of the tide.

From *Eaft-Teignmouth church* you will find another leading towards Dawlish, under the beetling arenaceous cliffs, where

  " Mufing onward to the founding fhore,
   The lone enthufiaft oft will take his way,
   And lift, with pleafing dread, to the deep roar
   Of the wide weltering waves."

On thefe cliffs, and indeed from every part of the hill that backs the town, there are many good views,—the fea, and the coaft terminating in the opening of Torbay,—the pleafing hills and vales of Stoke and Coombe, with a fic-quent dip into the river,—a part of the town, with the *Den*, and tiers of fhipping, fome building, others repairing,—and the oppofite village, are the moft diftinguifhing features

---

From TEIGNMOUTH *we ferry over to*

SHALDON,

WHICH lies near, and almoſt under, a promontory called the *Neſs* It is in much eſtima-
tion as a ſummer reſidence, and is viſited as ſuch
by many genteel families It contains ſome
good lodging-houſes, recently erected,—in fact,
the whole place, generally ſpeaking, conſiſts
of modern buildings, but the inhabitants not
being reſtricted to any regular plan of building,
the houſes are now ſeen to an evident diſad-
vantage, from their ſcattered ſituations; ſome-
times encroaching upon and interrupting the
proſpect and convenience of each other Not-
withſtanding this, it is a charming village, and
(public amuſements and promiſcuous ſociety
excepted)

excepted) is, in many points, fcarce inferior to its oppofite neighbour. SHALDON is the property of the *Right Honourable Lord Clifford*, and lies partly in the parifh of *Stoke-in-teign-head*, and partly in that of *St. Nicholas*, to whofe fweetly fecluded and picturefque chapel there is a charming level walk of a fhort mile, it is fituate a little above the river, encircled by fome venerable trees,

" Who, as they fhelter from th' annoying blaft,
Shut from the vacant gaze the rich repaft,"

in the hamlet of RINGMORE, which confifts of a few neat cottages, fhipbuilding, chiefly for the Newfoundland and coafting trade, is carried on to fome extent here.

Afcending a fteep hill from behind SHAL-DON, fome agreeable walks may be found on *Stoke* (or rather *Ringmore*) *common*, commanding ample profpects of the eaftern coaft, even to the chalky cliffs of the Ifle of PORTLAND. But the walk moft frequented is on the beach,

under

under the *Nefs*, which, as you approach the fea, higher rears its precipitous head The morning fcene this beach prefents you with is fublime,—the rifing orb, firft breaking thro' the glowing horizon, an immenfe globe of fire, gaining in glory as it advances, at times throws fuch an infinity of its hues on the fmoking ocean, that it almoft dazzles your fight, the luftre is, however, well relieved by the dark fhade of the jutting promontory, round which you may climb on the huge maffes of red grit the fcowling tempeft and the tooth of time have gnawed from the rugged fides of the parent rock, until you have loft fight of all traces of cultivation, and nothing but the fwelling bofom of the ocean receives your excurfive eye

The contiguity of TEIGNMOUTH and SHALDON, (being only feparated by the before-mentioned paffage, which is feldom dangerous) renders the rides of one equally applicable to the other

RIDES.

RIDES.

Various little excursions may be made for an hour or two, on horseback, on the healthy down of LITTLE HALDON, &c which we shall pass over, and hasten to those more attractive, advertising the reader, however, that there are other roads to and from the objects we visit, besides those which, for the convenience of seeing other scenes, we shall take The grounds and pleasant seats of *Mamhead, Oxton, Powderham,* &c may be seen in a day's ride, as well from TEIGNMOUTH as DAWLISH.

———————

Ride to LINDRIDGE UGBROOK PARK, *and* CHUDLEIGH,—*return by* KINGSTEIGNTON,— total about 16 *miles.*

On leaving TEIGNMOUTH we take the road to BISHOPSTEIGNTON, (i e. the BISHOP's TOWN, upon the river TEIGN) before whose antique church

church it paffes, the fimilarity of this ftructure
and that of *Eaft-Teignmouth church*, has been
already noticed; but this has to boaft a moft
beautiful ornamented arch, in the Saxon form,
thrown over the weftern entrance to the church.
Old Walls, as it is now called, claims our next
notice;—it was an edifice erected by *Bifhop
Grandifon*, for the reception of old and unbene-
ficed clergymen   His endowments were never
ill placed   they were not for the maintenance
of the drone, but for thofe whofe day of labour
had paft, and whofe means were infufficient for
the fupport of old age and decrepitude, and
who, moreover, from their facred function,
were incapacitated from fecular occupations,
was this hofpital raifed, the eaftern end of the
chapel, and the walls to the fouth, comprife
nearly the whole of what now remains of the
original building, its antiquity, if there were
no records to carry it back to the time of Edward the Third, in the beginning of the four-
teenth century, might be traced in the cor-
rodcd

roded ftones, its windows, and overfpreading ivy. The fouthern walls now form part of a large fquare inclofure, containing a barn, &c. and in the inner area is a farmer's yard. It is a poffeffion of the *Rev. Mr. Comyns*, of *Wood*, who is alfo lord of the manor of *Bifhopfteignton* From thence you proceed to *Lindridge*, a capital manfion, fituate in a rich lawn, beautifully wooded. The buildings, now in part taken down, it is recorded, once covered nearly an acre of ground, a room, preferved in the ftyle it was originally fitted up, conveys a fpecimen of the fplendor of its ancient inhabitants. The proprietor, the *Rev. John Templer*, has a valuable collection of paintings, by *Vandervelt*, *Vanbloom*, and other eminent mafters, which decorate its walls. From *Lindridge* a fheltered lane takes us to the turnpike road, at a fmall diftance from the gate of *Ugbrook*, the feat of the *Right Honourable Lord Clifford*, whofe noble

C

park

* A moft charming ride will be found through a delightful wood, leading from *Lindridge* towards Sandy-Gate.

park you enter by a ſtately avenue of luxuriant
growth; this is one of the moſt charming ſpots
Devon has to boaſt,—whether we trace the
ample walks, ſhadowed by the richeſt foliage,
—whether we follow the wild ſweeping vales,
adorned with beautiful hanging woods,—or
accompany the " flow, winding, deep, ma-
jeſtic flood,"—or whether,

> " Pleaſed, we turn and ſee the turrets riſe
> In rough majeſtic grandeur to the ſkies,"

we muſt agree with the poet, who ſo ably de-
ſcribes its beauties, that

> ————————" Collected here,
> As in one point, all nature's charms appear "

Leaving theſe happy ſcenes, by aſcending a
hill, (on which ſtands a direction poſt) you are
preſented with a pleaſant proſpect of the town
of Chudleigh, the vicinity of which abounds
with picturefque views, and to which we ſoon
deſcend Chudleigh is a ſmall town, diſtant
nine miles from Exeter, and about ſeven from
Teignmouth, and thro' it paſſes the road from
Exeter to Plymouth, which greatly contributes to enliven it, here are two inns, both

very

very good,—the *King's Arms*, and the *Clifford's Arms*. Near this town the *Bishops of Exeter*, (who procured a charter for a market, and two fairs for the place) had a magnificent palace, the remains of which are still visible. Proceeding on the *Ashburton road* a short half mile, you catch a view of *Chudleigh rock*, an immense mass of marble that rises towards the west, almost perpendicularly, with a bold majestic front, adorned by a rich vest of ivy, and stained by a variety of mosses, while out of the chasms of the rock an infinity of pendulous plants

" Stream in the wanton wind."

About midway down the cliff, is a large cavern, whose dreary intricacies may be pursued by those who have an inclination, the expedition being attended with some danger. There is a superstitious tradition, that a sort of fairies inhabit the gloomy recesses, (I do not, however, rank them with the disagreeables the explorer has to encounter) and to this day the labourers on the lime-kilns call it " the *pixsey*, or *pixie-hole*." A

rugged

rugged foot-path will attract the admirer of the *picturefque*, toward a romantic water-fall, the mufic of which fwells upon the ear, before the ftream that produces the found can be difcovered by the eye, which

> ———" Loft within the lab'rinth of the wood,
> Thro' tracks untried, now drives its roaring flood,
> In loud confufion, o'er the broken fteep,
> Abruptly pours, and dafhes down the deep,
> From crag to crag the tumbling waters bound,
> And foam, and fret, and whirl their eddies roun',
> The rugged bed of huge mifhapen ftones
> Beneath the rude tumultuous torrent groans;
> Whilft aged oaks, by wanton nature bred,
> O'er the deep gloom their thick luxuriance fpread"

Returning to the turnpike road, you pafs *Lucc'*, an excellent houfe, the property of *Lord Clifford*, whofe valuable woods enrich all its neighbourhood. It is now converted into a boarding-fchool for young ladies;—the advantage of poffeffing fo charming and falubrious a fpot, for a feminary of this defcription, is, of courfe, felt by the prefent tenant. Inftead of crofling the Trees, which foon meets the view, take the left hand road, by a mill, which brings you

at length to the turnpike-road from EXE-
TER to NEWTON BUSHELL, and having
paſſed *Sandy-gate*, a public-houſe on the road
ſide, diverge again to the left, thro' the village
of KINGSTEIGNTON, and follow the banks of
the river to TEIGNMOUTH

———

Excurſion from TEIGNMOUTH, *through* KINGS-
TEIGNTON *to* STOVER *and* BECKY-FALL, *re-
turning through* HIGHWEEK *and* NEWTON —
Total about 28 *miles.*

We now re-trace our laſt road, on the banks
of the TEIGN, which, ſpreading its ſmooth
ſheet beneath, receives the eye,—oppoſite you
ſee RINGMORE, and around it many a ſmoking
cottage, ſcattered among the fertile meadows.
Coombe Cellars, ſtanding in a moſt picturesque
ſituation, advances into the tide, and meets
your eye, while above it the tower of *Coomb-
in-teign-head church* gleams thro' the hedge-row
elms,—below the road lie the farms of *Wear,*

C 3   enjoying

enjoying a charming profpect of the river. KINGSTEIGNTON, to which you now arrive, is a fmall village, heretofore very much afflicted with agues; but the marfhes which contained the ftagnant water, that occafioned the difeafe, have now, for the moft part, been drained, and the pernicious *miafma* confequently removed.

The church has a good effect, with its grove of tall elms, feen from many points,—it has in it a tomb, on which the following is infcribed·

> *Richardus Achim*, hujus Ecclefiæ
> Vicarius, obiit *Feb.* 10th, 1670.
>   Apoftrophe ad mortem,
> *Damn'd 'tyrant!* can't prophaner blood fuffice,
> Muft priefts that offer be the facrifice?
> Go tell the *Genii* that in *Hades* lye,
> Thy triumphs o'er this *facred Calvary*,
> 'Till fome juft *Nemefs* avenge our caufe,
> And force this *kill-prieft* to revere good laws!

It would, perhaps, be difficult to produce an infcription parallel to this, and it certainly may be confidered as better adapted to a heathen cenotaph, than to a chriftian minifter.

Contiguous

Contiguous to the church-yard are the ruins
of what is fuppofed to have been a prebendal
houfe, and by it a mill, both very picturefque.
About half a mile from KINGSTEIGNTON, you
enter on *Teign-bridge*, the two arches of which,
that are thrown over the river, are conjectured
to have been built on fractured Roman buttreffes The Roman road from EXETER, over
HALDON, thro' TOTNESS and BRENT, into
CORNWALL, being traced to this fpot, ftreng-
thens the fuppofition,——on the right is a very
neat houfe, not a little ornamented by a noble
oak that grows on the oppofite bank of the
river,——fomewhat farther, on the oppofite fide,
are fome buildings, erected by *James Templer,*
Efq the proprietor of the adjacent canal, as
receptacles for the cubes of clay that are cut in
the neighbourhood, at the turnpike gate, one
mile from NEWTON, we follow the right hand
road, that takes us by the elegant church of
TEIGNGRACE, whofe blue fpire fhoots up, and
is a fine object from many parts of the fur-

C i   rounding

rounding country. *Stover Lodge,* the feat of Mr *Templer,* is an excellent houfe, built with granite, having a pleafant garden, and a hot-houfe attached to it, and overlooking a fine piece of water,—croffing BOVEYHEATHFIELD, on the left, lies a coal-work, which will draw the attention of the naturalift, it produces the *lignum foffile* common in fome parts of GER-MANY, there has lately been a fteam engine placed on it, to free it from the water that has for feveral years inundated the pit, by its fide a building is juft erected for the manufacture of earthen-ware, where, according to the pun of the country, " people burn their goods, and are never the worfe for it," nearer the town is another pottery, which has been eftablifhed many years at INDIO. Some part of the entrenchments vifible on BOVEYHEATH-FIELD, were thrown up and occupied by *Lord Wentworth,* who was defeated here by a detachment from the army of *Sir Thomas Fairfax,*

Fairfax, then blocking EXETER, and loft
400 horfe, 100 foot, and 6 ftandards, one
of which was the King's,—quitting the town
of BOVEY TRACEY, at its weftern extremity,
you proceed by a mill to fkirt up a moft romantic vale, and taking the left hand road on
entering the barren downs, you afcend to
MANATON, a fmall village, on a bleak but
romantic fituation, here nature works with
rude materials,—huge unwieldy ftones, and
rugged hills, covered with the "many-fingered
fern," are fpread around, while fcarce a tree,
that merits the name, is feen in the fences,
whofe very brufh-wood cringes and fhrinks
away before the prevailing wind. The fcathed
rock of *Haytor*, with a range of brown hills,
that fo frequently formed the diftance to our
coaft views, lies before us; this defert country
reminds us of the poet's defcription of SWISS-
ERLAND —

" No vernal bloom the torpid rocks difplay,
But winter, ling'ring, chills the lap of May "

From

From MANATON a lane conducts thro' a conti-
nuation of the fame barren country, and having
croffed the *Bec*, or rivulet, (a fynonimous term,)
a gate on the left opens into a wood, which
contains the ultimate object of our journey.
Should the rains have been favourable, and
fwelled the ftream to its banks, (as in time of
drought none of thefe mountain ftreams are of
confequence) the fatigue of the ride will foon
be forgotten. A cottage, which from its fituation amid this romantic and wild fcenery, is
a moft attractive object, offers a fhed for your
horfes, and one of the woodman's children may
be taken as a guide, tho' the contiguity of the
cataract precludes the neceffity of fuch a mea-
fure,—from the cottage you proceed beneath
trees, clad with hoary moffes, and by unwieldy
fragments of moor-ftone, to the fall, which
drives its torrent with great violence over a
heap of huge unconnected rocks, fometimes
parting and plunging into the interftices of its
wild bed, and at others, boiling up and preci-
pitating

pitating its tumultuous ftream from rock to rock, when having reached the foot, it " whirls its eddies round," and dafhing forward into the wood, is foon loft in the fombre maffes of its fhade Near this is a moft curious cavern, and not a great way diftant is the before-mentioned *Haytor rock*,—indeed the whole vicinity claims the attention of every eye that delights to perufe the fportive and romantic page of nature.

As it will be difficult for the ftranger to find his way from the vague directions of the peafantry, it will be moft advifable for him to purfue his road to the church of *Ilfington*, and from thence to get into the *Afhburton turnpike road*, midway between the fourth and fifth mile ftones, a gate opens into a lane on the foutheaft, near which, a path-way branches off leading to a moft remarkable oak, belonging to *Lord Clifford*, it lies about half a mile from the *Bovey* and *Newton road*, having eight large trunks

C 6

rising from one stool, forming a most stately head, and is well worth the attention of the curious —Before us

" The decent church that tops the neighb'ring hill"

of HIGHWEEK is seen, to which we soon ascend. HIGHWEEK (as the termination of *week*, *vic*, or *vica*, a village, denotes) was originally a Roman station; the vestiges of an encampment are still visible in a garden belonging to a farm called *Castle-ditch* This parish includes that part of NEWTON (which is our next stage) that has the adjunct of BUSHELL, or as it was more properly named BUSSELL, from a family of that name, who then resided at BRADLEY.

At NEWTON there are two good inns, the *Sun* and the *Globe*, it having nothing remarkable to boast, we may return by our former road to TEIGNMOUTH, or by the way of SHALDON, which our next route will describe

Excurſion from SHALDON *to* NEWTON, BERRY-
CASTLE, *and* TOTNESS, *returning thro'* IPPLE-
PEN, DENBURY, &c. *to* TEIGNMOUTH —
Total about 29 *miles*

From SHALDON we take the road before deſcribed to RINGMORE, having the river on our
right, the bank of which, (having paſſed two
or three farm-houſes) above *Aſhbrook bridge*,
preſents a charming proſpect. *Coombe Cellars*,
ſtanding on a neck of land, the fine ſheet of
water, the village of BISHOPSTEIGNTON, the
two beautiful farms of *Wear*, and the hills near
NEWTON and BOVEY, are the moſt diſtinguiſh-
ing features,—the village of COOMBE, (an ab-
breviation of *Coombe-in-teign-head*,) about half
a mile further on, has nothing remarkable in
it, if we except the *vicarage-houſe*, a neat and
ſingular building, the reſidence of the *Rev.
B W Wrey*, ſcreened from the noiſe and buſtle
of the road that paſſes beſide it,—beyond
COOMBE a lane to the left takes us to *Haccombe*,

a

a manſion belonging to *Sir Thomas Carew*, Bart. This, we are informed, " is the ſmalleſt pariſh in ENGLAND, as to the number of dwellings, which are two only, the *manſion-houſe* and the *parſonage*" " *Haccombe* enjoys very extraordinary privileges. It is not included in any hundred no officer, either civil or military, hath a right to take cognizance of any proceeding in this pariſh, and by a royal grant from the crown, it was exempted from all duties and taxes, in conſequence of ſome noble ſervices done by an anceſtor of the *Carews* "* Near the houſe ſtands a moſt picturesque chapel, behind which a wooded hill riſes, and is no ſmall ornament to the lawn, this chapel contains ſome very curious monuments of the *Carew family*, and that of *L'Ercbedicon's*, who married into it, on the ſouthern door are ſtill to be ſeen the remains of four horſe-ſhoes, ſaid to be taken off a horſe's feet that ſwam with one of the *Carew's* a conſiderable

diſtance

* Prince.

distance into the sea, and back again, whereby he won a wager of a manor of land. The chapel of *St. Nicholas*, at RINGMORE, is remarkably similar in its form to this, and was built also by one of this ancient and distinguished family. Ascending a hill, we are brought to a common called MILBER DOWN, from the summit of which there is a most extensive prospect. The meanders of the TEIGN, from *Teign bridge* to the *Salmon-Wear*, are plainly discovered, above it we see *Stover-Lodge, Ingsdon*, and the range of hills behind, farther to the right is seen HALDON, with *Lawrence tower*, and opposite the village of KINGSTEIGNTON, whose church is, as it were, embosomed in trees. At the foot of MILBER DOWN, is *Ford*, " a neat and fair house," built by *Sir Richard Reynell*, (third son of *Sir Richard Reynell, of Ogwell*,) an eminent lawyer, in the reign of King James the First, it is supposed on the scite of an abbey, that gave the adjunct of

ABBOT

Abbot to that part of Newton, fituate in the parifh of Wolborough.

In the year 1625, King Charles the Firft took up his abode here, with his fuite, and one day after dinner, in the dining-room, at *Ford*, conferred the honor of knighthood on *Richard Reynell*, of *Weft Ogwell*, and *Thomas Reynell*, his brother, who at that time was fewer to his Majefty's perfon, " in prefence of their wives, and divers lords and ladies, faying unto them, God give you joy " King Charles the Firft vifited *Ford* a fecond time, and *William*, Prince of Orange, afterwards King William the Third, of aufpicious memory, flept here, after landing at Brixham, in Torbay The daughter and heirefs of *Sir Richard Reynell*, married *Sir William Waller*, Knt general of the parliamentary forces, from the active part *Sir William* took in the commotions of his day, it is prefumed, he did not often refide at fo great a diftance from the metropolis It appears, however, from his " *Recollections*," that he built and endowed a *work-houfe*, for the poor of NEWTON-ABBOT, and erected a *market-houfe* there, as a palliative for his having unjuftly attempted to deprive the Yardes of BRADLEY of the benefits of the market. His daughter and heirefs, by her marriage with *Sir William Courtenay*, brought *Ford* to that noble family to whom it now appertains The houfe ftands in a lawn, retired from the road, and oppofite it is a fmall deer-park Beyond *Ford* is the " WIDOWE's-HOVSE," bearing this infcription on its front,—

" Ift ftrange a Prophet's Widowe poore fhovlde be,
  Yf ftrange then is the Scriptvre ftrange to thee "

It was founded by *Lady Lucy*, (wife of *Sir Richard*) *Reynell*, for the reception of four* poor clergymen's widows, each of whom receive alfo an annuity of five pounds per annum, built on a charming fpot, overlooking

the

---

* The Feoffees have altered the original inftitution, and have divided it among two only, each receiving 10l per annum.

the TEIGN, and a fine fweeping wood* that runs to the water's edge, with the *clay-cellars* of *Hackney* in front, and part of KINGSTEIGN-TON village.

Paffing through the town of NEWTON ABBOT, and following the *Totnefs road*, we view on the right *Bradley*, and foon after, on the left, *Wolborough church*, feated boldly on a hill This church is what is termed a *donative*, being the individual property of *Lord Vifcount Courtenay*, under the infpection of the grand metropolitan alone,—it exhibits a good fpecimen of gothic architecture, of a light and airy conftruction, the chancel contains a handfome monument of *Sir Richard Reynell*, of *Ford*, who, with his wife and children, are reprefented at full fize in ftone, much of the primitive chafte fimplicity of the tomb has been deftroyed by profufe gilding and colouring. By its fide is the pew belonging to the clergymen's widows before fpoken of, over which

is

* From whence the oppofite view was taken

is a curious account of the neceffary qualifica-
trons they are to poffefs, and the rules they are
to obferve to entitle them to the refidence and
annuity —" *they fhall be noe gadders, goffuppers,*
tatlers, tale-bearers, nor given to reprocheful words,
nor abufers of anye   And noe man may be lodged
in anye of ye faid houfes, nor any beare, ale, or
wyne, be fould in anye of ye faid houfes, &c."

This edifice was once decorated with
" Stoned windows richly dight "
The late worthy rector, the *Rev. W Hugo,*
carefully collected whatever could be found
worthy of prefervation, and diftributed it in a
fanciful manner among the different windows,
giving each fome part.

Proceeding on the turnpike road to a direction poft, nearly three miles from TOTNESS,
a lane to the left leads to that noble ruin, *Berry-*
caftle, which we fhall have occafion to vifit,
and fpeak of hereafter, and for the prefent
continue

continue our ride to TOTNESS. The veftiges of the Roman road are ftill to be traced here, this town was once environed with a wall, and had four gates, tho' the fouth-gate is the only one now in exiftence. It was defended by a caftle,* built, it is faid, by one of the *De la Zouch* family, on a mound raifed for the purpofe, the walls of it, mantled with ivy, are ftill extant, and affume a venerable appearance. The people of this town were fo remarkably loyal, that in the reign of George the Firft, they prefented an addrefs to his Majefty, wherein they begged his acceptance of four fhillings in the pound land-tax, and alfo affured him, if the fervice required it, they would freely add the other fixteen,—but the chief boaft of TOT-NESS is the noble river DART, which runs at its foot, this river has its rife on the foreft of DARTMOOR, the fource of moft of the DEVON-SHIRE *ftreams*, at *Cranmere pool*, from a large morafs

* Some afcribe the building of this caftle to *Judhael de Totnais*, who erected a caftle, alfo. at Dartmouth.

morafs of brown fibrous peat; about two miles from its fpring, it divides, the moft confide-rable of its branches running by *Two Bridges,* an inn on the moor, and *Prince Hall,* the pro-perty of *Sir Francis Buller Yarde Buller,* Bart the confluence of the two ftreams is named *Dart-meet,* where once ftood a moft romantic bridge, formed of huge fragments of rock, fupported by others placed perpendicular, parts of which are now to be feen, and are here, (as higher up at *Poft-bridge,*) well worth the attention of the curious traveller. The river paffes from thence near *Spuchwick park, Lady Afhburton's,* and *Holve Chace,* on which is beautifully fituated a *Lodge* belonging to *Sir Bourchier Wrey,* Bart. the fcenery round which, rocks, woods, &c is picturefque and romantic in an uncommon de-gree. The holly trees affume a peculiar charac-ter on this fpot. Purfuing its way, it fkirts the extenfive woods of *Buckland,* where Mr. *Baftard,* Member of Parliament for the county, has a beautiful cottage, and to which, at a vaft expence,

expence, (hewn thro' the rocky ftrata which thruft themfelves into the DART) he is conducting a moft charming road.—Dafhing its waters beneath *Holne bridge*, the ftream meanders thro' fine hanging woods, until it approaches the venerable ruins of *Buckfaft Abbey*, which claim the attention both of the antiquary and the painter. Thence paffing underneath *Dart bridge*, over which the road from ASH-BURTON to PLYMOUTH lies, it foon enters a fine range of verdant meadows, often befprinkled with the foliage of fome rich coppices, and every mile increafing in confequence, having paffed *Staverton bridge*, where the fcenery is highly picturefque, it winds around the fine and elevated woods of *Dartington*, the ancient houfe of which ftanding on a rifing ground near the church,

—————————" O'er the level plain
Of fpacious meads, with cattle fprinkled o'er,
Conducts the eye ———————————
Where far beyond, and overthwart the ftream,
That, as with molten glafs, inlays the vale,
The floping land recedes into the clouds."

This is a ftately pile, with a quadrangle in the
middle, of nearly an acre, it was evidently
divided into diftinct tenements of yore, and
tradition reports the knights templar as its original inhabitants. It contains a fingular hall,
of large dimenfions, and alfo fome capital
paintings, brought by its proprietor, *Arthur
Champernowne*, Efq from ITALY. The DART,
below DARTINGTON, is, in many parts, ex-
tremely picturefque, it winds from thence
to TOTNESS, and is navigable from below
the bridge to DARTMOUTH.

Retracing our former fteps, about three miles
on the *Newton road*, we now diverge to the
left, thro' the village of IPPLEPEN, and proceeding thro' a quiet fhady lane, reach that
of DENBURY, (fo called, we are informed,
from being the burial-place of a hoft of Danifh
invaders,) and pafs before the retired feat of
Thomas Taylor, Efq Somewhat farther on you
have a view of *Ogwell-houfe*, an elegant modern

dern building, the refidence of *Colonel Taylor*, who poffeffes fome curious relics of carved work, originally belonging to the *Reynell* family, and that of *Holbeam*, whofe houfe once ftood in the parifh of OGWELL The road winds from thence, at the foot of hills, barren with refpect to herbage, but enriched with immenfe quarries of marble, ornamented with lime-kilns, and crowned with a fpiry obelifk Croffing the river LEMMON, at *Cherricombe-bridge*, we enter a moft delightful vale, and having advanced a few yards in the fine grove, a charming retrofpect between the trunks of the tall trees awaits,—the cottage by which we entered, the bridge we have juft croffed, an orchard behind, the back ground formed by a fine coppice of oak, and beyond it an eminence, on which rifes a fquare tower, finifhes the view The road, with a pleafing curvature, continues by the banks of the fportive ftream, thro' the grove. On the left hand "the waving wood," in full luxuriance, fpreads its rich foliage, and clothes the steep from the bottom of the dell to its apex,—on the other side the stream, the scene is quite changed, and the eye is surprised at the contrast,—a rude hill rises to an immense height, out of the barren sides of which grey rocks issue, and nod tremendous over the murmuring stream. After contemplating the rugged ridges and romantic shape of the abrupt eminences, we may almost imagine an *Alpine* scene offered to our view, and fancy may complete the illusion, by suggesting the wild *Chamois*, bounding from crag to crag, in the place of the peaceful flock that browse its scattered herbage, this grand landscape continues for some distance, a limekiln, with its huge mass of rock towering behind, only diversifying the face of the wood, and even increasing both its picturesque beauty and grandeur. The reader will, I hope, pardon the egotism of the following lines, and excuse the author's partiality for scenery, amid which he sometimes enjoys a happy hour.

D   *Written*

Written in BRADLEY VALE.

HAIL shades belov'd! where pleas'd my infant feet
Have often stray'd your beauteous scenes among,
Ere yet your hills my artless notes did greet,
Ere yet I tun'd my rude unletter'd song.

Ere yet I knew *Misfortune*'s ruthless train,
Ere pale-ey'd *Sorrow* pour'd her heart-felt tide,
Or felt the *iron family* of *Pain*,
Or bore the galling, scornful glance of *Pride*.

The downy hours flew softly o'er my head,
And as I wander'd sportive, chearful, gay,
New pleasures still their balmy influence shed,
And still succeeding, chas'd the old away

And where are now the joys I once did share,
Say, to what halcyon region are they flown!
Your spires, your woods, your vallies still are here,
The fleeting joys I mourn, alas! are gone!

When Memory kindly opes her blooming page,
And holds the faithful tablet to my view,
Her magic characters my soul engage,
Her devious steps my eager feet pursue

' 'Twas here,' she points, ' beneath this aged oak,
Our young associates pass'd the jocund day,
Or drew the minnow from the babling brook,
Or join'd tumultuous in some busy play.'

' If

' Up yonder copſe, that riſes from the vale,
Joyous we toil'd the cluſt'ring nut to gain ;
Or on a feaſt of berries to regale ,
Or cull the noſegay from the flow'ry plain.'

Au happy days !—what can the world ſupply,
To recompenſe the ſweet it ſteals away ,
Not Fortune's favours equal bliſs can buy,
Nor can promotion happineſs repay

Tho' now forlorn,—yet muſing in your glades,
I cheat ſome gloomy, melancholy care,
And ſlowly pacing thro' your ſilent ſhades,
Enjoy that ſacred calm that ſoothes deſpair.

————∞0030∞————

Winding up a ſteep aſcent, by the ſecond
lime-kiln, a ſhort diſtance out of the road, to
the left, is *Broadridge plain*, which will amply
repay a momentary deviation, the ſummit diſ-
playing

———————————————" the grace
Of hedge row beauties numberleſs,—ſquare tow'r,
Tall ſpire, from which the ſound of chearful bells
Juſt undulates upon the liſt'ning ear,
Groves, heaths, and ſmoking villages remote "

To which we add the gleaming river, which is

ſeen

seen gliding with majestic pace to its estuary, the town of TEIGNMOUTH, with its shipping, and the broad expanse of ocean flanking the whole. Without advancing from the spot that commands this prospect, turn towards the *west*, and a complete rural scene meets your eye, the opposite hills, with their projecting rocks, and the gazebo on them, the rich inclosures on the right, the vale beneath the wild meanders of the LEMON, lost at length by interposing eminences, and a smiling hamlet, encircled by orchards, are the principal objects.

Bradley, to which we now descend, is a well suited companion to the valley in which it stands, and is, perhaps, the most ancient seat, not at all modernized, in the county. The gateway is the most striking feature externally, the arch is semicircular, and over it is a Gothic window, this stile of architecture often occurs in ancient edifices, the heavy Saxon supporting the lighter Gothic. A chapel, long disused,

forms a part of the internal building. The
whole of the pile is kept in good repair by the
poffeffor, *Thomas Lare, Efq*. and perhaps a
more picturefque fituation is rarely to be met
with. Following the courfe of a mill-ftream,
we again enter the ftreets of NEWTON BUSH-
ELL, and return either to SHALDON or, by
croffing TEIGNBRIDGE, proceed on the oppofite bank to TEIGNMOUTH.

R de from TEIGNMOUTH to TORQUAY

The next ride (of about fix miles) will be
to TORQUAY, the laft fubject of our prefent
defcription. Ferrying over to SHALDON, we
climb the fteep afcent that leads to *Stoke common*, the higher part of which, for diverfity of
profpect, and a difcrimination of beautiful objects, will be rivalled in few counties. Beyond the common, on the coaft lies MINI-
COMBE, or MINNOW COMBE, where, opening

to a fmall cove, are feated, in a moft fe-
queftered manner, among a few fertile paftures
and orchards, half a dozen farm-houfes. Farther on, and oppofite a direction-poft, is the
road to *Whatcombe rocks*, the firft you pafs is a
bold perpendicular cliff, charnelled and wrin-
kled by time, round its rugged head the ftragling
ivy (its hoary locks) hangs pendulous, in many
a lengthening line and implicated wreath,
from hence the vale defcends rapidly towards
the fea, where it ends abrupt Here an immenfe cliff rifes, whofe fummit is fringed with
brufh-wood, and mid-way from the ocean appears darkling a vaft cavern, overhung by
beetling rocks, turning at the bottom of the
dell, towards the right, you have another view
of the horrid fiffure, and in front, fome detached rocks, of the moft fingular and grotefque forms, it feems to have been a fpot
where nature has fuffered fome vaft concuffion,
which defaced the fmooth furface of the vale,
and fhattered its rocks into huge fragments

Not

Not a tree is to be feen in this folitary place, its contiguity to the fea, and bleak expofure to every ftorm, has checked all vegetation, the ivy is the only plant that appears to thrive, and the wild genius of the place has traced its branchy clufters with inimitable tafte, and blended its deep verdure, with the grey tint of the rocks, with a highly pleafing effect. Rejoining the road, we proceed to the hamlet of *Mary church*, the tower of which is a moft confpicuous object for many miles round,* the road is frequently fprinkled with cottages, on the fronts of fome of which myrtles fpread in great luxuriance, and a few neat new-built houfes, which gives a chearful afpect to the country The village of Tor, or more properly Tor-Mohun, ftands on an eminence, and overlooks part of the bay The church is fituate under a ridge of rocky hills, in a pleafing

D 4 feclufion,

---

* Near this is *Shiplay*, the feat of the *Rev Thomas Kitfon*, one of the magiftrates of the county, feated low, and tho' too much fheltered for modern tafte, yet correfponded with that of our anceftors.

feclufion, furrounded by fences of fine elms,
the hills round Tor are of a remarkable fhape,
thro' the verdant turf of which many fanciful
crags project from the fummit to the foot and
the vales are richly covered with foliage
The defcent to Torquay particularly boafts
this fcenery, on the left are feen fome rugged
conoidal hills, almoft barren, and on the oppofite fide the rich groves of *Tor abbey* receive
the eye By the turnpike-gate rifes a grand
quarry of lime rock, with the kiln below, and
on the right is a regular row of neat cots, with
each a fmall garden, wafhed by a brook of water in front, and fomewhat further on the other
fide, are feveral modern built lodging-houfes,
nearly as pleafant as thofe on the beach, fhort-
ing a wooded hill, being free from that difa-
greeable that the receffion of the tide leaves,
tho' undoubtedly the latter have great advan-
tages at other times, from the variety of ob
jects continually floating in their view, as well
as fome tranfient beauties that may not luckily

be

be caught by an accidental walk   The moft
pleafant fituation is, however, occupied by five
or fix lodging-houfes, defended from the furge
by a parapet wall, which, interpofing, precludes the view of the naked beach, and admits
a profpect of the fleet, when at anchorage in
Brixham road   The inns are the *Crown and An-
chor*, and the *London Inn*, they are but tolerable

TORQUAY

WAS once the property of *William Lord Brewer*, the founder of *Tor albey*, and afterwards purchased by *John Ridgeway*, who refided here, it now appertains to *Sir Lawrence Palk, Bart* Member of Parliament for the county of Devon, and *George Cary*, Efq It is a pleafant village, in a fmall retiring cove of TORBAY, which takes its name from the circumjacent hills and rocky eminences or tors, and was the grand rendezvous of our immenfe fleets, during the late war The whole curve of the bay is computed at twelve miles, from the extreme point of which (called *Hope's Nofe*) TORQUAY is about two miles diftant, fheltered from the violence of the waves by a protruding ridge of rocks

The

The air of this place is in general very sharp and does not agree, consequently, with every constitution, but in point of romantic beauty and picturesque scenery, TORQUAY, and its environs, are rarely to be surpassed, and to a lover of simple nature, (who can dispense with crowded assemblies, gaming-tables, and a train of luxurious refinements,) will afford a most agreeable *sejour*, during the summer months. The invalid, also, may rest assured of finding the lodgings and accommodations good, (for a place yet in an infant state) the people are remarkably civil, and not addicted to impositions. The bathing-place is at a little distance from the village on a soft, secluded, and sheltered beach, but it furnishes only one machine at present. TORQUAY, before the war, as well as other sea-ports on this coast, was concerned in the Newfoundland trade, which is again reviving with the return of peace.

WALKS.

W A L K S.

One of the many romantic *promenades* of the neighbourhood, will be found north-east of the quay, following a foot-path across a field, and into a common, plentifully sprinkled with shrubs and furzes, the combination of whose tints produce an agreeable effect, beneath stretches the fine bay, to which the various shipping, and airy skiffs, give a charming animation, and several abrupt chasms, discovering a small beach below, occasionally vary the scene. The appearance of *Tor abbey* from hence, is very fine, as well as the whole sweep of the coast, terminating in *Berry head*, beyond which the ocean spreads its cerulean waves On these hills, in the season for mackerel and herrings, many a solitary group of fishermen may be seen, intently eyeing the shoals of fish that approach the shore To diversify the walk on your return, a green-sward foot-path will take you to a sequestered lane, from

whence,

whence, a few fields diftant, the ancient manor-houfe of *Torwood* prefents itfelf, and the vale opening towards the fouth, difclofes a part of TORQUAY, in a different (tho' equally as pleafing a) character, from what is cuftomarily feen   The water, by the intervention of a wooded knoll, is entirely excluded, *Waldon* rifes behind, crowned with firs, and the old feature of *Haytor rock* bounds the horizon

———

Walk to TOR ABBEY.

Afcending a flight of fteps, behind a row of lodging-houfes, you are led to a very fteep, rugged foot-path, made a little more than half way up the hill of *Waldon*, whofe foot is covered with many huge maffes of detached rocks, and whofe precipitous fides are decorated with an abundance of pendulous plants and variegated fhrubs, the view it affords of the quay

opposite,

oppofite, the remarkable hills beyond, and the opening of the bay, is truly beautiful

Emerging from this craggy road, the fmooth-nefs of the enamelled meadow is

> " Like velvet neat,
> Soft to the eye and to the feet."

Near the receding angle of the wall that divides *Waldon*, above the foot-path, is an (apparently accidental) aperture, over which a large ftalk of ivy has wreathed a fantaftic arch, thro' which is feen a pretty grotto, covered with mofies of various tints, this wall bounds a charming inland profpect, compofed of the village of Tor, and its fmiling paftures, and that curi-ous building *Tor chapel*, perched upon the fum-mit of a ridge of rocks, it was once an appen-dage to the *abbey* before us, and as it has never been defecrated, nor even applied to the ufes of the reformed church, it is fometimes vifited by the Roman Catholic crews of fhips lying in the bay Croffing a lane, we now enter the

lawn

lawn, and view the manfion, furrounded by tall avenues of luxuriant growth, it is a large building, confifting of a centre and two wings, fronting the moft charming part of the majeftic bay, TORQUAY no where forms a prettier picture than from hence, nor do the furrounding rocky torrs appear to greater advantage *Berry bead*, and the roadfted for the grand fleet, are in full profpect, with the circuitous fweep of the fhore, adjoining the weftern wing is a fine caftellated gate-way, (coeval with the ancient abby, that occupied the feite of the prefent houfe,) fortified with octagonal towers and battlements, under the femicircular arch of which is now to be feen the fculptured arms of fome one of the abbots, beyond this gate-way is the original barn, belonging to the ancient monaftery, it is altogether of a Gothic caft, overfpread with a venerable mantle of ivy, and decorated with loop-holes and numerous buttreffes The Roman Catholic chapel attached to the houfe, is ornamented with a fuperb altar

and

and paraphernalia, on each fide of which aie paintings, one ieprefents the crucified Saviour; the other the bleffed Virgin The end of this chapel, piojecting into the garden, is completely vefted with ivy, there aie alfo fcveral ruins, clad in the fame elegant diapeiy, among which we difcover a laige Norman aich, with a fmall one on either fide, richly adoined with fculpture.

William Lord Bruer, we before noticed, founded this abby, in the ieign of King John, beftowing upon it confide able ievenues, his fon greatly added to thefe donations, and, among other lands, gave *Ilfham,* in this paiifh. *William Lord Bruer,* the fecond fon of the foundei, dying without iffue, his poffeffions were divided among his five fifters, and *Aliuia,* the youngeft, bringing to her hufband, *Reginald de Mohun,* Tor, it fiom that time loft the appellation of *Bruei,* and acquired that of *Mohun,* which it ietains to this day At a

fmall

fmall diftance to the fouth-eaft, is a fort of rocky ifland, approachable at low water, fepe-rated from a projecting cliff by the fea, cor-roded by the faline fpray in the upper parts, and undermined and excavated by the furge below, the loofe fandy ftratum has formed it-felf into rude natural arches, from which you have feveral charming views, as the rocky pil-lars divide the landfcape, *Tor abby*, and its wooded vale, appear to much advantage, but the opening towards TORQUAY is, perhaps, more beautiful ftill. A few yards farther on produces another curiofity, of fomewhat the fame nature,—here, to an immenfe cavern, there are three entrances, two lateral, and another in front, the roof may be near 30 feet high, and the length 150 feet, on the fmooth perpendicular face of the back of this cave, there is another opening, leffening in fize as it recedes from the view, exhibiting, from the firft principal entrance, a fine per-fpective, under thefe clifts are a number of

pools,

pools, conftantly full of fea water, that contain various forts of polypi, and other marine animals, fome of the former are of a confiderable fize and ftriking beauty, exhibiting the vivid colours of the fineft anemone.

Ride from TORQUAY *to* NEWTON BUSHEL.—
Total 15 miles.

Taking the road oppofite the quay, we are brought, amid undulating hills, to *Torwood*, a fine old building belonging to *Sir Lawrence Palk*, and ftanding in a very pleafing fituation; about half a mile beyond this, a gate, facing the road, opens into a fpacious field, the lower part of which, (a coppice) contains that celebrated cavern, *Kent's bole*, the aperture of which is not of any great magnitude, and is almoft fhrouded in bufhes. As I was, a few months fince, procuring a guide, to explore

the

the gloomy recefs, (I mention the fact as a caution to the unwary) a young naval officer, attended by a labourer, with a lantern, tinder-box, &c. overtook me, who, accofting me, obferved, if I would accompany him, " *he hoped to fhew me a refurrection*," at my entreaty he explained himfelf, by faying that five of his brother officers, belonging to a fhip in the bay, had that morning entered the cave, without the precaution of taking a guide, and had carried with them a quantity of portfires, the voluminous fmoke of which had extinguifhed the only candle they had; and when their momentary glare was exhaufted, they were left almoft fuffocated with fmoke, in total darknefs; having exhaufted their ftrength and patience in fruitlefs efforts to find the way out of its dreary intricafies, they gave themfelves up to defpair, when he, having parted from the reft, guided by his good genius, at length emerged into the cheering light of day. Having augmented our guides, we entered the chafm, with

each

each a candle, and cautiously proceeded, as it
was remarkably rough, and would fcarcely al-
low fufficient height to ftand erect; after a
fhort defcent, it opens into a fort of hall, more
fpacious and lofty, the blaze of our lights dif-
fipating enough of the gloom to expofe the
ponderous jaws of many a horrid orifice on
either fide, our path now became fomewhat
fmoother, and permitted us to examine the
many whimfical petrefactions and incruftations
nature had fecreted in thefe Cimmerian fhades,
on the approach of the light to the roof, in-
numerable gems fparkled as it paffed, with
beautiful radiance. After fome time, the unfortunate objects of our fearch anfwered our re-
peated fhouts, and, directed by the found, we
found the difconfolates, feated round the mar-
gin of a limpid pool, (whofe waters forbad a
farther difclofure of its fecret receffes) almoft
exhaufted with fatigue, but the happy profpect
of a releafe, from what they had almoft con-
cluded would have been their grave, gave them

new

new animation, and I foon had the pleafure of congratulating them on their return to the woild, from which they had been more than fix hours fecluded.

Beyond this is *Ilefham*, an ancient houfe, formerly belonging to the abbey of *Tor*, in the yard of which ftands an uncommonly fine cln, one of the buildings, much dilapidated, from the appearance of a bell, that was evidently raifed above its roof, feems to have been a chapel. From hence we climb a rugged road to Babicombe, and looking down, perceive fome cottages clung, as it were, to every ledge that afforded level fpace enough to ftand on, rifing tier above tier, the fcenery of this little hamlet is uncommonly romantic,—rocks of an uncouth fhape and huge dimenfions, being interfperfed with the cottages, and fometimes frowning over the roof, or fupporting the foundation, below, the chain of cliffs is interrupted by a fmall pebbled beach, and oppofite is the

fine

fine quarry, known by the name of *Petit Toe*, producing a beautiful coloured marble. Paſſing thro' the village of MARY CHURCH, a left hand lane takes us to BARTON CROSS, and in a ſhort time to MILBER DOWN, where the road divides nearly in two equal parts an encampment, probably firſt thrown up by the Romans, and afterwards occupied by the Danes, who changed the original ſquare, which the Romans uſually choſe, into their own faſhion, that of an oval, what ſtrengthens this conjecture, is a ſmall one higher up, that ſtill retains its paralellogramic form, which the Danes, poſſibly, never had occaſion to uſe. The proſpect it commands

" Of hills and dales, and woods and lawns, and ſpires,
And glittering towns, and gilded ſtreams,"

ſhould not be paſſed over in ſilence. Proceeding by *Ford*, and the *Widow's Houſes*, we enter the town of NEWTON BUSHELL, from whence we may explore the beauties of *Bradley Vale*, and to vary the route, return thro' the

village

village of KINGSKERSWELL, by a very pleasant road, to TOR, and from thence, by the church, to TORQUAY.

———◆———

Excursion to COMPTON-CASTLE, BERRY-CAS-TLE, *and* TOTNESS, *from whence, down the river* DART, *to* DARTMOUTH, *and return thro'* PAIGNTON, &c.

Leaving TORQUAY, we pass thro' the lower part of the village of TOR, and by the gate and fine avenues of *Tor abbey*, and having reached the first hamlet beyond, a right hand lane takes us to COCKINGTON, by the parish church of which is a fine stone-built mansion, the residence of the *Rev R. Mallock*, erected on the spot where once stood a house belonging to an ancient branch of the *Cary* family, and from thence to *Five-lanes turnpike-gate*, where we deviate from this road, and descend to the

village

village of COMPTON, at the higher extremity of which ſtands *Compton-caſtle* We find *Compton-caſtle* was, at an early period, given by the *Lady Alice de Pola*, unto *Peter*, who took the name of *Compton*, from the place, and continuing in that family ſeveral deſcents, came to the *Gilbards*, or *Gilberts* It is now the property of *James Templer*, Eſq and contends with *Haye's farm*, near EXMOUTH, for the honor of being the birth-place of *Sir Walter Raleigh*; the ſketch given of it excludes the modern alterations, barns, ſtables, &c. which, tho' excellent of their kind, greatly derogate from its picturefque appearance and grandeur The front, towards the north, with its tower, gateway, (once furniſhed with a portcullis) and machicolations, has a ſtately air, to which the Gothic window of the chapel, and the remaining battlements, greatly contribute. The back part of the ruins are very picturefque,—the venerable ivy, twining round and ſupporting the dilapidated walls of the once proud apartments.

ments, gives an awful gloom to the fpot, which even the view of the part inhabited does not diffipate,—to our furprize, we here difcover the remains of a geometrical ftair-cafe, which evidently denotes this curious contrivance to be known by our anceftors We return from thence thro' the village of MARLDON, the church of which contains a ftone infcribed to the memory of the before-noticed *Peter de Compton*, and rejoin the turnpike-road, from which, about two miles diftant, a lane branching off to the right, conducts us to a fmall hamlet, that very opportunely offers a fhelter for the horfes, and following the footpath, we wind through a venerable wood, that fcreens the folemn ruins of *Berry caftle*,

> " Which on a dark hill, fteep and high,
> Holds and charms the wand'ring eye "

The gate-way and its tower, of which a fketch is given, are nearly the whole of the remains of the baronial caftle of the *De Pomerois*, who came to ENGLAND with the Conqueror, and

E   who,

who, for their good fervices, had no lefs than fifty-eight lordfhips beftowed on them. Here, at *Berry*, did *Radulph de Pomeroi* feat himfelf, building this caftle, which, from its advantageous fituation, muft have been impregnable in thofe days, it occupies the whole of a projecting eminence, that terminates towards the north abrupt, at a great height above the glen. Towards the eaft and weft, the fall of the ground is fo rapid, that it is all but perpendicular, the only part thereof that was acceffible was on the fouth, and this was defended by a ftrong gate-way, which was poffeffed of a double portcullis, within the wall was a large quadrangle, but the original ftructure, on every afpect, (excepting the fouthern) has been fupplanted by other buildings, and even thefe are haftening to decay The caftle, and its precincts, were fold, about the year 1550, by *Sir Thomas Pomeroi*, to *Edward Seymour*, Duke of *Somifet*, whofe defcendant, *Sir Edward Seymour*, inheriting the caftle, and his

father s

father's predilection for the romantic fpot, be-
gan a moft magnificent edifice, within the
walls, which was never completed, notwith-
ftanding the immenfe fums, tradition reports,
were expended on it. *Berry caftle* may be confidered as a fcene of unrivalled beauty. The
antiquary and the painter muft here unite in
admiration, and the latter might multiply his
fketches *ad infinitum*, for, in every afpect, where-
foever he places himfelf, he will meet with
fome peculiar difcriminated beauty,—the ru-
inous walls, and the noble trees that rife in fuc-
ceffive majefty up the fteep afcent, affume a
new appearance at every turn of the road, and
the diverfity never permits the attention to
flag, or the admiration to ceafe. The fcreen,
on the right, as you go down the dell, confifts
of hills, nearly as high as thofe on the oppofite
fide, and they are either clothed with fine
hanging woods, or fcarred with rough rocks of
grey-tinted marble.

A

A pleasant road, of about two miles and a half, brings us to TOTNESS, where, crossing a long narrow bridge over the DART, the traveller will find a very comfortable hotel, called the *Seven Stars*

From TOTNESS, a most pleasant water scheme offers, for ten miles, down the DART,—on every turn of this majestic river, a charming scene presents itself to the eye,—at some places taking the appearance of a bason of water, at others, of a long extended lake, the banks frequently clad with the richest vest of foliage, from the edge of the stream to the towering summit, and decorated with some of the most beautiful villas classic taste has erected, until we arrive at the rocky shores of DARTMOUTH This last town is seated on the sloping side of a hill, with some very romantic eminences opposite, it contains a few good modern houses, and a number of ancient ones, its streets are incommodiously narrow, the lower tier of houses

Houfes having communication with thofe above them by flights of fteps In the town are the venerable walls of an old caftle, rifing immediately above the water, and at the entrance from the fea, it is defended by another caftle, on the walls of which a few cannon are mounted. This fort has a very picturefque appearance, together with its neighbour, *St Petrock's church*, from the lower part of the town, and indeed any part of the harbour Somewhat above, on the cliff's edge, are the remains of a caftleated edifice, ivy clad, and much dilapidated, probably built by *Judhael* The cliffs and this caftle form a moft romantic picture from the fea We find the amazonian prowefs of the females of DARTMOUTH upon honorable record, for having beaten back fome French troops, (who, egged on by the hope of plunder, invefted the place,) and making the General, and part of the army then prifoners Ferrying over to KINGSWEAR, we remount our horfes, and at the fummit of a hill, nearly two

E 3

miles

miles from DARTMOUTH, find a road leading to *Nethway*, a very neat house, belonging to J *Fowndes Luttrel*, Esq the proprietor of that beautiful seat in the north-west of SOMERSET, *Dunster castle*. At the turnpike-gate we branch off to the right, and with many a pretty catch of the sea before us, enter the upper (or *church*) town of BRIXHAM, near the higher extremity of which, a lane to the left conducts us to that curious reciprocating spring, called *Lay-well* the period of its ebbing and flowing is irregularly varied, having been known to rise and fall from once to nine times in the space of an hour *Brixham Quay*, famous for the landing of William the Third, about one mile beyond, is the most populous place, and has a good hotel,—the *London Inn*,—from the circumstance of having been so frequently visited by the grand fleet, it has thrived much during the late war Those who are fond of military improvements, will be gratified by a visit to BERRY-HEAD, on which stand some excellent barracks, forts, batteries

&c

&c erected of late years, for the defence of the *Bay,* which before was wholly at the mercy of the enemy.

Returning to the town of BRIXHAM, we quit the turnpike road for that of *Lupton,* enter a gate near a lime-kiln, which is decorated by a beautiful old afh tree, and winding thro' fome cultivated fields, to the angle of the garden wall, we gain the firft view of the fine clumps and plantations that crown the rifing hills, which appear to interfect each other at agreeable points, and by a handfome gate, enter a luxuriant fhrubbery, that judicioufly fcreens the out-buildings *Lupton-houfe* is a ftructure of confiderable elegance, the fouthern front being peculiarly handfome, and ftands in an excellent fituation, environed by pleafing eminences, hung with flourifhing woods, (which *Sir Francis Buller,* Bart the proprietor, is increafing) and well watered vales We rejoin the turnpike, at a fhort diftance from the neat village

village of CHURSTON, and paſſing the ſix-
mile ſtone, (from DARTMOUTH,) take the right
hand road for PAIGNTON, at the entrance of
which, a modern built houſe ſtands prettily,
above the road. Near *Paignton church,* which
is itſelf a very handſome edifice, are the remains of an *epiſcopal palace,* formerly belonging
to the *Dioceſe of Exeter,* but alienated by *Biſhop
Voyſey,* the gate-way is yet ſtanding, and the
whole ruins bear evident marks of grandeur,
particularly a part exuberantly veſted with ivy,
to the ſouth-weſt of the church, where the di-
menſions of a magnificent apartment may be
traced, the part in the higheſt preſervation is
uſed as a barn, and thatched, the whole area
was encloſed by a wall, battlemented, and
adorned with loop holes, at the eaſtern angle
of which, a tower, built, probably, as well for
the charming proſpect it commands of the noble
bay, as for defence, ſtill

" Smiles at the tempeſt, and time's ſweeping ſway "

The road from thence, thro' luxuriant vales,

pirmits

permits many a pleafing glimpfe of the fwelling tide, intermixed with rural fcenery, and
we foon retrace our former fteps to TORQUAY,
where, having explored

> " ———— The varied view
> Of rocks, amid the fun-fhine, tow'ring dark,
> Of rivers winding wild, and mountains hoar;
> And caftle gleaming on the diftant fteep,"

we leave the wearied traveller to his repofe.

F I N I S.

TREWMANS, PRINTERS, EXETER

CPSIA information can be obtained
at www.ICGtesting.com
Printed in the USA
BVOW04s1751230717

490048BV00005B/13/P

9 781140 989752